To My Friend
Mattie Hopkins
With all good wishes!

Let's Get
Together
On Earth
Before Taking Off
On The Road To Heaven

May God continue to
Bless you now and always

~ Al Hall ~

Feb. 11, 2015

Let's Get Together On Earth Before Taking Off On The Road To Heaven

Poems

A L   H A L L

iUniverse

LET'S GET TOGETHER ON EARTH BEFORE TAKING OFF ON THE ROAD TO HEAVEN

iUniverse books may be ordered through booksellers or by contacting:

iUniverse
1663 Liberty Drive
Bloomington, IN 47403
www.iuniverse.com
1-800-Authors (1-800-288-4677)

Because of the dynamic nature of the Internet, any web addresses or links contained in this book may have changed since publication and may no longer be valid. The views expressed in this work are solely those of the author and do not necessarily reflect the views of the publisher, and the publisher hereby disclaims any responsibility for them.

Any people depicted in stock imagery provided by Thinkstock are models, and such images are being used for illustrative purposes only. Certain stock imagery © Thinkstock.

ISBN: 978-1-4917-3941-9 (sc)
ISBN: 978-1-4917-5949-3 (hc)
ISBN: 978-1-4917-3942-6 (e)

Library of Congress Control Number: 2014921695

Printed in the United States of America.

iUniverse rev. date: 01/13/2015

This book is dedicated to

Dr. Mabel Hall Pittman Middleton
Jackson, Mississippi
My high school English teacher

Sybrina Fulton and **Tracy Martin**
Parents of
Trayvon Martin

This book is also dedicated to

people who are responsible for positive change in the world,
worshippers, musicians, seniors, church ushers,
young people who are trying to find their way, and
anyone who has been, or wishes to be, in love.

Contents

Acknowledgments

Thanks to those who provided invaluable feedback and encouragement during the production and publication of this book. My sincere gratitude goes to everyone who assisted in any way. I would like to give special recognition to the following:

Reviewers
Reverend Samuel Nixon Jr.—Alexandria, Virginia
Dr. Sedric Roberts—Fort Washington, Maryland
Minister Lisa Bailey-Harper—Alexandria, Virginia
Charles Perkins—Lanham, Maryland
Tazh Hall—Tallahassee, Florida

Technical Support
Johnny President—Springfield, Virginia
Djawa Hall—North Palm Beach, Florida
iUniverse Staff

The Author's Photo
Earl Stafford Sr.—McLean, Virginia

Artistic Consultants and Interior Design
iUniverse Staff

Cover Design
Earl Stafford Sr.—McLean, Virginia
Rania Nazhat—Fairfax, Virginia
iUniverse Staff

Foreword

What a refreshing experience to delve into the poetic framework and tapestry of life that Deacon Al Hall offers in this work! He brings us "up close and personal" to our observations about life! This poetic field of bursting imagery dances into our minds and hearts in a most revelatory and engaging way. To treat the aspects of thought and controversy around President Barack Obama, open up the context of happiness and sorrow, and lift up in tribute those among us who have made and are making a difference is expressed in a most exciting and creative flow of thought and rendered text. This work brings out many dimensions of our black church experiences, from the admiration of cooking to the significance of sin and salvation. Deacon Hall treats men's ministries, music ministries, and love at the altar in an almost whimsical yet sobering and sound manner, while he lifts up matters on Capitol Hill, challenges to young people, and how to cancel a frown with a good laugh in a creatively exhilarating manner! This is a must-read for anyone who appreciates fine writing in very inviting style! Feel the Spirit as you enjoy this work in God's grace and love!

—Reverend Samuel Nixon Jr., 1998 Diamond Homer Famous Poets Society Award; Famous Poet for 2000; Associate Minister, Alfred Street Baptist Church, Alexandria, Virginia

Preface

I wrote this book of poetry to encourage people to spend more time trying to get together on earth before taking off on the road to heaven. Several issues in today's society inspired me to move forward with this project.

People often pretend to be concerned about those who are facing various undesired challenges but do absolutely nothing to help them. Many churchgoing people are so busy trying to get to heaven that they have no time to do anything beneficial for people on earth. There are young people today who are disrespectful to those around them, while others are disrespected and even criminalized just because of what they wear or who they are.

Inasmuch as I have had the experience of knowing that a good laugh can cancel a frown, I have shared several poems that introduce humor as a way of lifting readers from the pits of despair. We may not always be joyful, but we certainly don't have to spend all of our days on earth tangled in a web of sadness. If we can find a little time for laughter, perhaps we can reward ourselves and others with a season of opulent happiness.

Although obstacles continue to rise in relationships, people are still falling in love. Therefore, I have included poems that reveal the pleasure of being involved in the wonderful institution of marriage and the agony of disappointment when things go wrong.

Our measure of success in whatever we do is frequently built on the foundation already laid by those who went before us, many of whom have gone on to their eternal rest. We need to remember them, as well as those young people whose lives were snatched from them before they had an opportunity to make their contributions to the world. This book contains tributes in memory of them.

We can see happiness all around us until those inevitable days of sorrow creep into our lives. This is when we should realize that all of us are standing under one canopy of life that shelters us on rainy days and sunny days. We never know which will come our way next. Therefore, we need to be able to lean on each other in a spirit of unity; otherwise, all of us may eventually fall together.

Oh, Come! Let's Worship the Lord!

Welcome to the Worship Service

We welcome you on this glorious day.
Both the pastor and congregation are glad you're here.
We are honored that you came to worship with us
On this special Sunday of the year.

We have gathered in this place for a specific purpose,
And we trust that you feel the same.
We are here to worship a loving Savior
And sing praises unto His holy name.

We hope you already feel at home.
He is waiting for your personal call.
Everybody is somebody in God's house.
Jesus gave His life to save us all.

If you are just visiting in our city,
We hope you will enjoy your stay.
We ask God's blessings as you return home.
May He guide you every step of the way.

If you are now moving to this local area,
You don't need to feel all alone.
When the invitation is extended to you,
Come forward and make this your home.

We know you will be blessed by the sermon today.
Some of the music you have already heard.
Please sing praises, enjoy the service,
And get ready to hear a powerful Word.

A Tribute to All Church Ushers

*The author was commissioned by the Alfred Street Baptist
Church Ushers' Ministry in Alexandria, Virginia, to
write this poem for their Annual Ushers' Day.*

When we decided to become ushers,
We thought it would be a joy to serve.
No one gave us the slightest hint
That people can press your very last nerve.

Seating is nothing new to most of you.
You know exactly how things are done.
Yet, we've had a hassle every Sunday
Since our service was first begun.

Please help us do what we are trained to do.
Help us to make each service worthwhile.
Help us in getting everyone seated,
And we'll keep thanking you with a smile.

There may be space between you and your neighbor
Who is sitting on your left or right.
Would it hurt for you to move either way,
Although it may be somewhat tight?

Even when there are those "big crowd" days,
We know what we are supposed to do.
Our greatest challenge can be made a lot easier
If we can get a little support from you.

Please stop looking the other way
When you see the ushers gazing down your pew.
Somebody is going to be asked to move over
And, most likely, it's going to be you.

Oh, we know when you're trying to ignore us.
Yes, we see you when you roll your eyes.
That doesn't bother us at all anymore,
Because experience has made us wise.

You can see clearly that space is limited.
The situation couldn't be much worse.
So why on earth do you occupy one seat
And take another one for your luggage-size purse?

That heavy coat looks right for the season.
Its material may have been caught by a trap.
But please don't drape it over the back of your seat
To hang in somebody else's lap.

The person sitting behind simply adores you,
But they could admire you even more
If you would carefully fold your nice coat
And place it in front of you on the floor.

Don't have ill feeling about the ushers.
We are in no way trying to be mean.
Don't worry about your coat getting dirty,
Because the floors are extremely clean.

That round-top Stacy Adams or godfather hat
Resting on that big Bible makes you no winner.
The Bible and the hat don't need to be saved.
So release that seat for some poor lost sinner.

Some of you come in late and bring three guests.
You want them to see your clout.
But there are no seats for any of you,
And all of you have to march back out.

Ushers may suggest that you go to overflow.
That is the best they can offer as a treat.
But if you hang around trying to argue with them,
You could end up not getting a seat.

Don't depend on your friend to text you.
Your seat has not been reserved.
Arriving on time is the magic key
As some of you have already observed.

We thank those who arrive real early.
They walk right in and find their places.
They always look quite comfortable
With smiles on all of their faces.

You can have that very same look,
Although you may not have it yet.
Everyone knows that if you have the right spirit,
A smile is not that hard to get.

Now just because you arrived early
Doesn't mean that you own the pew.
You may have to do the "Alfred Street squeeze,"*
Because sharing is what we've learned to do.

You may start thinking of unkind words
Since you have nothing better to do.
Be careful what come out of your mouth,
Because it could be a great reflection on you.

So do try your best to cooperate.
There is no need to start a fuss.
If you simply follow the ushers' directions,
Things will be better for all of us.

---

* "Alfred Street squeeze" is a term used to encourage worshippers to sit closer together to provide more seating in the sanctuary.

You arrive at eleven thirty or even twelve o'clock.
This may be your personal trait.
But since most people were seated by ten forty-five,
You should know, by now, that you are late.

Some complain to the ushers about parking.
You feel that you just can't take it anymore.
Other people have the very same problem.
So check that hostility at the door.

Come on in prepared to worship.
We offer a smile for your personal woes.
Brace yourself for a biblical sermon
That just may happen to step on a few toes.

You ask us to find a seat for you.
Our interest in responding is keen.
We walk all the way to the seat and turn around
To find that you are nowhere to be seen.

It is not a whole lot of fun for ushers
To keep walking and standing on our feet
When your only contribution to the worship service
Is that of complaining about a seat.

Now, we get up early on the coldest morning
So that we can be here to serve at eight.
You stay in bed and want to give us grief
Because you decided to sleep a little late.

It doesn't matter where you are sitting,
Whether in the sanctuary, balcony, or overflow.
When the pastor says, "The doors of the church are open,"
It does not mean "You should get up and go."

That means "Come and receive the joy of salvation,
Find a new church home, or repent of sin."
So please stay where you are for a few more minutes
Until the choir has sung the final "Amen."

We don't mind collecting your Communion cups,
Because that is one of the things we do.
But when you have a bulletin, please take it home,
Because it is something that belongs to you.

You stick it over behind those hymnals,
As if it means nothing to you at all.
And Monday morning before ten o'clock,
You are giving the church office a call.

"Where is this? What time is that?"
It's something you could already know.
It would be in your phone or on your calendar
If you hadn't been in such a hurry to go.

Thanks for celebrating this occasion with us.
You have made this a wonderful day.
We will keep on doing our best to serve.
May God bless you in every way.

The Fervent Prayer

Experiencing the power of prayer is awesome.
That is one reason we can continue to pray.
We should pray for our friends, as well as our enemies,
And we should thank God every day.

We sometimes pray our fervent prayers
And rush petitions to God without hesitation.
When He is not rushing at the very same speed,
We may get a feeling of separation.

In weak moments, we may not pray at all
Because no answer seems to be coming our way.
But do we ever stop to give serious thought
To what it is that we have to say?

Is there a reason why we hear no answer?
Are we connected to God each day?
Is our personal relationship to God intact
As we try sending those prayers His way?

It's natural to think of blessings that others receive.
We don't know *why* they started praying or *when*.
They may have been getting things right with God
While we were still bogged down in sin.

Are we letting God direct our lives?
Or do *we* always know what is best?
Do we take charge of most important tasks
And then see if *He* is able to handle the rest?

God knows all of our concerns in life,
From the greatest to the small.
He has promised to be with us always,
But we should honor Him enough to call.

There are times when we forget to give God thanks.
When disappointed, we turn in disgust.
Yet He continues to show us His love.
So we should be willing to wait and trust.

It is not our duty to correct God's promise,
And He has promised to see us through.
He does not falter on His commitment.
What He says, He is sure to do.

So let us pray with confidence.
Let our words come straight from the heart.
Let us continue lifting up our fervent prayers
Or decide this is the day to start.

Keep Blessing Me with Your Love

Lord, You know my thoughts.
You know all my words and deeds.
You know my sincere desires,
And You know everything I need.

Take charge of my whole life, Dear Lord.
Keep blessing me with Your love.
Protect me from my enemies
Until I reach my home above.

I love You, and I trust You, Lord.
I've trusted You many times before.
I want to keep on serving You
So I can love You even more.

I'm Trusting in My Savior

I'm trusting in my Savior.
He is my true friend.
He will always love me.
His blessings have no end.

Oh, what a wonderful Savior!
How great to know His voice.
I have found a friend forever.
King Jesus is my choice.

I'm glad I have a Savior
Who lifts me when I'm down.
He will always love me.
What a true friend I have found!

Lord, We Need Your Touch

Touch our eyes, Lord,
That we may see more clearly
Your will for our lives.

Let us not walk blindly
As if we are in a world of darkness.

Touch our hearts, Dear Lord,
That they may have more
Compassion for those in need.

Help us in our quest to show
More love for one another.

Touch our ears, Lord,
That we may hear the Word
As Your servants deliver it.

Help us to be doers of the Word
And not hearers only.

Touch our feet, Lord,
That we may move forward
To tell others about Your love.

Strengthen us in our willingness to
Tell what You have done for us.

And touch our lives
That we may set good examples
For those around us to see.

Let everything we say and do
Magnify our Lord and Savior Jesus Christ.

Amen.

Jesus, My Lord, I Love You

What can I offer to Jesus Christ?
What can I do today?
What do I have that's good enough
For the price He chose to pay?

Chorus:
Jesus, My Lord, I Love You.
Jesus, My Lord, I Love You.
Jesus, My Lord, I Love You.
You are the Eternal King.

I can give my praise to the Savior.
I can lift my voice in song.
I'm not worthy of the blessings
He gives me all day long.

Jesus, My Lord, I love you.
Please take these gifts I bring.
And keep on blessing me, Lord.
You are the Eternal King.

Where do I turn in sorrow?
Who is my refuge in grief?
Knowing that Jesus will help me
Brings joy and sweet relief.

I Praise You, Lord

Oh, Lord, You're my rock.
You're my fortress and my protector.
You're my shield.
You're my shelter.

When I was in trouble and
Didn't know what to do,
I remembered to pray,
And, Lord, I called on You.

You scattered my enemies
In a way that all could see.
You reached down from heaven,
And then You rescued me.

You caused my feet to run
And caused my hands to fight.
You are a faithful God,
And You're all right.

I Praise You, Lord.
I Praise You, Lord.
I Praise You, Lord.

Follow Ezra's Example, and Open the Book

Quite often, without taking time to think,
We deliver some kind of strong expression.
We never realize that we have hurt someone,
So we see no need to make a confession.

Ezra stands before the congregation.
Things are being done in a certain way.
There is a response to him by the people of God
As they listen to what he has to say.

When he opened the Book, the people stood.
When he blessed the Lord they said, "Amen, Amen."
They lifted their hands to the Almighty God,
Who could forgive them for their sins.

All of the people bowed their heads
With their faces turned to the ground.
They worshipped the Lord in spirit and truth.
Oh, what a joyful sound!

God's Word will last forever.
It has existed throughout the ages.
To find what it says to all of us,
We will have to turn the pages.

Conversations by God's people deteriorate,
Whether they are in the east, west, north, or south.
That is because people fail to open the Book
Before they decide to open their mouths.

If you know you are going to start talking,
Ezra has given a major clue.
Before you utter a single word,
Follow his example of what you should do.

Open the Book each day, and seek God's guidance.
Ask Him to guide you with your talk.
We should ask Him to always direct our paths
As we continue our Christian walk.

Why Are You Blocking the
Door to Heaven?

Why are you standing there in the way?
Don't you have anything else to do?
There may be someone who wants to pass,
But first, they have to get around you.

Are you trying to block the door to heaven?
If you stumble, things will not go well.
While you're trying to block the door to heaven,
You could fall backward right into hell.

I think it would be better to help someone.
Isn't there something that you could say?
People are lost, and they need the hand
Of someone who can show the way.

Look around you and see the crowds.
There may even be many more.
They all want to get a glimpse of heaven,
But you're standing there blocking the door.

Who asked you to take that position?
I wonder if you can dare to tell.
You had better stop blocking the door to heaven
Before you fall backward into hell.

Everybody you know is full of sin.
They will never see the face of God.
You won't try to help them see the Light.
You never give them a positive nod.

Just keep standing there blocking the door.
That is a task at which you excel.
You may realize the error of your wicked ways
When you end up way down in hell.

There is still time for you to make a change
If heaven is where you want to dwell.
People who won't do right while facing heaven
Can fall backward and land in hell.

A Good Laugh Can Cancel Your Frown

They Preached Him up to Heaven

This man had lived a sinful life,
Seven days out of seven.
But just as soon as he kicked the bucket,
They preached him up to heaven.

They told about how he'd been so good
And how he treated his fellow man.
They forgot about how he never shared
And never gave a helping hand.

They went on and on with compliments
About the man who would always give.
Perhaps it's good they didn't remember
The way he really lived.

They had speakers from all around
With selected words they wanted to say.
Not one of them would dare to mention
All of the debts he refused to pay.

The man was lying quietly in his casket,
Wondering, *Who could this angel be?*
He said to himself as he shrugged his shoulders,
They couldn't possibly be talking about me.

Is a Little Red Ant Interrupting Your Life?

Do you ever go looking for things too big?
Do you overlook the little things close by?
Do you spend too much time on the big picture
And miss the small things in your eye?

The elephant is a powerful animal.
He is known to be big as well as strong.
He can conquer some of the greatest foes,
Facing the enemy all day long.

He doesn't worry much about other animals.
He is not frightened by the poisonous plant.
But the elephant is simply horrified
At the thought of facing a little red ant.

The elephant is proud of all his power.
He is able to trample each harmful plant.
But he can't stop the stinging inside his trunk,
If it is caused by the little red ant.

You may be president of a corporation.
You could become head of a technology plant.
But don't let your career be completely destroyed
By the presence of a little red ant.

Do you ever worry too much about big stuff?
Do you seem to miss what you could very well see?
Is your focus set on things too great
When a little moderation may be the key?

You may do well by trying to reach greater heights.
You may succeed in having reasonable gain.
But don't fool around and be completely subdued
Because the little red ant is inflicting pain.

A Dedicated Member of Bedside Baptist

I'm tired of getting up to go to church.
In fact, it's extremely tough.
So until I have a change of heart,
Bedside Baptist will be good enough.

Sometime I have to sit in the back.
I can't seem to get to church on time.
I don't have this problem if I stay in bed,
And my wide-screen TV is divine.

Sometime the choir is too loud at church.
It seems that my eardrums begin to pound.
If I don't like the volume on the television,
I am in control of turning it down.

Deliver me from services that last too long,
And that's almost every time I go.
I don't have this problem at Bedside Baptist.
I can switch channels and watch another show.

I've heard that I should be with other Christians,
But that is advice I cannot heed.
I can use a lot of things on Sunday morning,
But mingling with people is something I don't need.

Friends say it would make my pastor happy
If I could just let him see my face.
Well, I greet my pastor every Sunday
By saying, "Good morning, Reverend Pillowcase."

Another advantage of attending Bedside Baptist
Is that I can check the sales and rush to the store
I don't need any guidance from the ushers
To find the appropriate exit door.

I can make a stop with Brother Seasonal Clearance.
I can shake Sister Discount's hand.
If Dr. Mark Down happens to be on duty,
I can get an early start with Mr. Layaway-Plan.

Every now and then, I may go to church,
But I enjoy television worship alone.
So until there is a startling revelation,
Bedside Baptist is my church home.

I Can't Keep Dragging Holiness Around

I decided to join the church last Sunday.
Now I can also start looking sad.
It seems that half of the people there
Have experienced something bad.

They encouraged me to come and join them.
Now they sit in their seats and frown.
I guess the load gets extremely heavy
When you are just dragging holiness around.

I've heard from some that the Christian life
Brings happiness in every way.
They tell me that being a Christian
Gets much better each passing day.

I think I'll find this happy group
Who enjoy praise and a joyful sound.
They're not tired and feeling burdened
From dragging holiness around.

Now that I'm in this fellowship,
I have no reason to just sit and frown.
I'm going to live a life of happiness.
I just can't drag holiness around.

I'm going to smile at people wherever I go.
I'm going to wave like I'm wearing a crown.
I refuse to get in the rut with others
Who are just dragging holiness around.

Come on and let's join that happy group.
The experience should be something profound.
Instead of dragging holiness from place to place,
Let's start spreading the gospel around.

Choir Director's Communiqué

This communiqué includes both humorous and serious lines "borrowed" from various church choir directors. Some lines were written exactly as the directors delivered them. Others were changed for poetic effect.

Dear Choir Members,

All of you know when rehearsal starts.
I'm so pleased that you remembered the date.
You have certainly come to the right location,
But you need to improve on this arriving late.

Some of you are late, and you've been missing rehearsal.
You're either out of town or you're out in space.
But if you don't practice the two weeks before we sing,
Go into the congregation and find your place.

It's not fair to those who come every week
And work hard for the allotted time.
Then you come walking in on Sunday morning
Thinking everything should be just fine.

That's not the way it's done these days.
You wouldn't like it if this should happen to you.
We're all responsible for doing our part
And it really doesn't matter who.

Now we're going over a familiar piece.
How many have seen this song before?
I really should stop asking that question,
Because your denial increases more and more.

We've done this song at least three times.
Last December you learned every word.
Now you claim it's all new to you
And act like it's something you've never heard.

Okay, breathe and sing the notes clearly.
Obvious errors are something you cannot hide.
You have to move smoothly into the next measure.
So please don't attempt to slide.

When I tell you to breathe and sing,
That is exactly what I expect of you.
Since God has blessed you by giving you breath,
Breathing is the least that you can do.

Come on, everybody, we are singing harmony!
I said that as we were about to start.
And as soon as we get past the first two lines,
You decide that you are going to sing parts.

Now, I'm not here to embarrass anybody
But most of you are not beginners.
If this section over here keeps missing rehearsal,
I'm going to find me "Three Mo' Tenors."

You altos are singing way too high.
That should be easy for you to see.
If that is the key in which you insist on singing,
With the sopranos is where you should be.

I'm sure there's a place in that section for you,
Because some sopranos are singing in a real deep voice.
Please make up your mind where you are going to sing
And do it while you still have a choice.

What is wrong with you basses and baritones?
You act like you cannot hear.
Who is that singing way down low
When I am playing notes that are way up here?

How many of you have your tape recorders?
I saw you flashing them as you came through the door.
You must not listen to them when you get home,
Because you are just as wrong as you were before.

Tell me please, what else I can do
To help you basses try to understand?
I suppose you want me to play it louder
When I'm hitting the keys as hard as I can.

How many tenors understand what I'm saying?
You must get those notes up and out of there!
I want you to try singing way up here
As if it's coming up out of your hair.

Now, some of you are talking when you should be listening.
There is a price you will to have to pay.
When it comes your turn to sing the very same measure,
You'll be asking, "What did the director say?"

You need to memorize your music, people.
You're looking east, west, north, and south.
Some of you will look anywhere you can,
Trying to snatch the words from somebody's mouth.

You cannot expect the director to keep feeding you words.
What will happen if the director is not there?
Your mouth will be open with nothing coming out
Because you haven't tried to do your share.

I want all of you to put the music down.
It's exactly the same as the very first line.
Why is your head buried down in the music
When we've been over this for the fifteenth time?

Why do you think I'm standing in front of you?
All you have to do is sing and watch me.
Some of you are still singing after I cut you off,
And that's something that should not be.

A lot of you altos are just making up music.
I won't single you out, but I must note it.
You know who you are, and I'm here to remind you
That is not the way the composer wrote it!

You are not singing what I'm playing?
Please stop and take another look.
I do know how to read this music,
And that is exactly what's in the book.

I do want all of you to sing your best,
But you should make some effort to blend.
You should not be the only person whose voice is heard,
So let's see if this loudness can end.

When I say, "Get softer," I don't mean "Stop singing."
Stay in tune, and bring your voices down.
There is nothing melodious about every line
Being sung in the loudest sound.

All of you need to show some life.
You're standing like a bunch of artificial plants.
Put some life into this uplifting song
And stop treating it like Gregorian chant.*

Why can't you sway with everybody else?
From out here that's an awful sight.
It looks sort of funny when you're going left
While everybody else is going to the right.

Now what is that you sopranos are singing?
Don't make me go into a musical rage!
I can't imagine where you're getting your version,
Because I don't see that anywhere on this page.

All of you had better pay attention,
Because we will practice on into the night.
I don't care how long it takes.
We are going to stay here until we get it right.

You are not getting the notes, baritones!
I want every last one of you to stand.
Sing it the way you hear it being played
Unless you have a more convincing plan.

I have no idea what you are saying, choir.
You sound like you're speaking Binglish.
Let's try singing that measure again,
And this time, let's try it in English.

---

* Gregorian chant is music that was named for a leader of the Catholic Church,
Pope Saint Gregory the Great (AD 590–604). It is usually sung in Catholic
churches in unison and without accompaniment. The text is primarily scriptural.

There are a lot of things you don't know.
There are musical things that you cannot do.
But everybody should know at least one thing:
That is, whether or not you even have a clue.

So get some idea of what you're supposed to sing.
That responsibility is one that falls on you.
I can tell by the looks on some of your faces
That you feel like most of the songs are brand new.

When the song is one that you don't know,
You should reduce your singing speed.
Don't go jumping way out in front,
Because you are not qualified to lead.

There is more to being in any choir
Than just standing there with a lot of poise.
We need you to make some effort to sing,
In addition to making a joyful noise.

Please fix your mouth so the sound comes out.
Shape your lips so they are up and down.
If your lips are widened from left to right,
You will not produce a pleasant sound.

That's much better, but we must stop now.
I thank you so much for coming to sing.
When you really give it all you've got,
You realize the joy that music can bring.

Last Sunday, the congregation was spiritually uplifted!
A blessing came from God through you.
You sang so joyfully, and you were in the Spirit.
That put the worshippers in the Spirit too.

We thank each of you for working so hard.
You continue this from week to week.
Hard work is sure to bring praise to God
And bring us memories we can always keep.

Continue to enjoy singing and praising the Lord.
Let us honor Him in all we do.
We wish you peace, love, joy, and happiness.
It is a blessing to serve our Savior with you.

Sincerely,
Your directors

I'm Trying to Get to Heaven

I'm working on my ticket to heaven this morning,
So please don't get in my way!
I have no time for anything earthly.
You'll have to catch me on another day.

I'm trying my best to get to heaven.
Drunks and the homeless are not in my scope.
Addicts and poor people are time consuming.
They may never find peace and hope.

I am not responsible for any of these.
My Savior is somewhere waiting for me.
I'm sorry I can't be more hospitable,
But this is just the way it has to be.

I don't have time to hear your problems.
That's something that will slow me down.
I don't have time to deal with small things.
Right now, I'm heaven bound.

I'm on my way to church this morning.
I cannot help you with your flat tire.
I'm going to sing praises to God,
So helping you is not my desire.

No, I can't drop you off at your church.
You will have to stand around here and wait.
Perhaps someone else will give you a ride,
But I just don't believe in arriving late.

I'm too busy with my church concerns,
So please try your best to understand.
There may come another time in the future
When I can lend you a helping hand.

A Tribute to Members of the Senior Ministry

If you are eligible to join the Senior Ministry,
There should be no further hesitation.
Your quality of life will be enhanced.
That is factual and not speculation.

You won't be sorry about the fellowship.
Participation may give you a lift.
We are glad to be known as seniors.
We are flexible, and we know how to shift.

Some of you are busy around your home
Or you're always on the run.
Come and join the Senior Ministry,
And get ready to have some fun.

It's not going to make you one day older,
And you're not getting younger by staying out.
Face reality, and enjoy Christian activities.
You will enjoy it, and there's no doubt.

Seniors thoroughly enjoy gathering to eat.
No sugar or salt is what the doctor said.
We ask the question among ourselves,
"What's going on inside that doctor's head?"

If the Culinary Ministry prepares peach cobbler
Or if it happens to be a nice coconut cake,
Seniors are going to eat it—just to be sociable.
If it's offered, it's something we'll take.

After a recent fabulous luncheon experience,
Someone said, "This is a blessing from above."
One senior made a personal observation,
Declaring, "It's almost like being in love."

Seniors have been accused of carrying aids.
Well, nationwide, the accusation is true.
As you increase in age, you may realize
That you will be forced to carry aids too.

You may be adjusting *hearing aids* in the morning.
There may be *Rolaids* before retiring at night.
There may be *Band-Aids* for our cuts and scratches
And *medical aids* to keep our bodies upright.

You may see seniors arriving with walkers,
Or you may see folding canes.
That doesn't keep us from joining activities
That exercise the body and brain.

You don't need to feel sorry for seniors.
And please don't describe seniors as old.
There may be at least a few in the group
Who won't mind getting you told!

We are often called seniors or seasoned saints.
There are other names you may have heard.
We are quick to forgive and excuse mistakes,
But *old* is simply not the chosen word.

Midday Bible study, followed by lunch,
Should cause you to rise and get on your feet.
But it's not too cool if you skip the study
And then show up in time to eat.

We're inspired by Dr. Judy Fentress-Williams.
For our Bible study, she's always there,
She not only teaches the Holy Word,
She provides time for us to pray and share.

Getting some of the things we desire as seniors
Is never, for us, a difficult task.
We have already learned from years of living
That we should not be too proud to ask.

Reverend Marcia Norfleet has great plans for us.
We are the best seniors she has ever met.
The more we cooperate and show our love for her,
The more special favors we're likely to get.

Periodically, she invites guest speakers,
And as soon as the speaker begins to talk,
Some of us decide this is the time
For us to get up and start to walk.

Do seniors talk during the speaker's presentation?
Oh, we are experts at doing that!
If the speaker has everyone else's attention,
That's when seatmates often start to chat.

Sometimes it may appear to you
That seniors' movements are just a little slow.
But seniors know how to step it up
In ways you may never know.

If you're talking about Alfred Street seniors,
Be careful how you use their names,
Because they will let you know in a second
That bingo is not their only game.

Now a few seniors claim their knees are aching.
They say that it's hard to get around.
But when they hear the music for line dancing,
They know how to get on down.

Seniors hold on to their independence.
And they may even start a little fuss.
They often drive their personal chariots,
Leaving others to ride the church bus.

Events may look as if they are shaping up nicely.
The planning committee says things are going fine.
As soon as they make the final arrangements,
Seniors exert the authority to change their mind.

Seniors give every detail when telling long stories,
So your listening may start to diminish.
They may repeat what they have already said,
But they are not stopping until they finish.

We appreciate the respect you show for us.
We love you for all you do.
Just keep on living and one of these days.
You may become a senior too.

So please continue to honor the seniors.
And don't link our action to any past position.
Just say, "Seniors have a severe case of *enjoying life!*"
We call it a *preexisting condition.*

If you still have reservations about joining the group,
Wait for a great leader to show you how.
Pastor Wesley could be at the head of the line
In exactly nine years from now.

I Am Certainly More Holy Than You

Now you think you've become so holy.
What more bragging can you do?
You talk about your fancy religion,
But your actions don't follow through.

I'm tired of your flaunting your holiness.
Remember that I claim to be holy too.
As a matter of fact, it just might be
That I am more holy than you.

You say you go to church every Sunday,
And you sing in a choir or two.
I go Sunday as well as Tuesday night.
That makes me holier than you.

You take Communion every first Sunday.
You say you always take the bread and cup.
But when I see how you live throughout the week,
I say you just do not measure up.

Besides, I take Communion twice a month.
This practice is not anything new.
You can see who's ahead with this ritual.
This is additional proof that I'm holier than you.

Let me tell you about your holiness.
For you, there is very little hope.
Nobody on earth is holier than I
Unless it is His Holiness, the pope.

So Glad to Be a Baptist

I am so glad to be a Baptist.
And I will be one until the day I die.
But there is one thing that I must admit.
I don't know the reason why.

Perhaps it's because my parents are Baptists.
Maybe it's because real Baptists like to eat.
Is it because some worship while standing and clapping
And others worship sitting in their seats?

We think members should be baptized by immersion.
Open communion is something in which we believe.
If there is something asked in the name of Jesus,
Those who are sprinkled will also receive.

There are those who participate in the immersion process,
But there is one point they don't seem to get.
If the heart is not right when they go down dry,
They are still sinners when they come up wet.

I understand there are Baptists of different kinds.
I'm just not able to sort this whole thing out.
No matter how hard I look for the contrast,
My mind remains clouded with a lot of doubt.

I could be Primitive Baptist or Progressive Baptist.
Southern Baptist is something else I could be.
I guess I could be Missionary Baptist.
It doesn't make a lot of difference to me.

There are a lot of things Baptists have in common.
In many areas their differences appear.
I'm just going to keep on being a Baptist.
I think my mind is now murky clear.

Can You Trust Your Secondhand God?

Have you bought anything that was secondhand?
Did it turn out to be all right?
Or did it decide to leave you stranded
In the middle of a cold, cold night?

How do you feel about things already used?
Do you feel the same as if they were new?
Does it matter whether it's something old?
Does that make any difference to you?

You may like things that belong to you,
Not something used by somebody else.
If they can find what they need in life,
You can find the same thing for yourself.

So why keep clinging to your parents' Salvation,
When you know they have a personal claim?
They have accepted a gift from the living God,
And you can now accept the same.

Your parents have already repented of sin.
They have made a decision to be baptized.
They cannot repent for you, my friend.
This is something you should recognize.

Mom's Christianity belongs to Mom.
And Dad's belongs to Dad.
You must accept your own gift of Eternal Life
If this is something you have never had.

Section III

Poems for Men's
Ministry Celebrations

The author was commissioned to write poems for
Special Men's Ministry activities at
Braddock Baptist Church and Alfred Street Baptist Church in
Alexandria, Virginia, including
annual men's retreats and the father-and-son banquets.

Dwelling Together in Unity

In the beginning, there was God's creation.
Heaven and earth were made by His hands.
In His creation, there are men of God,
And here we are united to stand.

Thank God for those who labor in love
That is genuine and heavenly sent.
Thank Him for the men of Alfred Street
And all of the families we represent.

Praise God for guiding as we strengthen our unity.
Thank Him for both the joy and pain.
We know that, "Unless the Lord builds the house,
The builder only labors in vain."*

We men have a torch for the lost to see.
It is something that we should not hide.
We have endured in our church and family life,
Because the Good Lord has been on our side.

Our sons and grandsons are in God's care.
Future generations will pass this way.
As beacons of light, we are focused on God,
And this is where our focus must stay.

Alfred Street men should be rejoicing.
The Good Shepherd has guided His sheep.
God has never failed to keep His promises,
And there are some that we must also keep.

-----------------------------------.

Psalm 127:1

How pleasant it is for us to dwell in unity!
It is so wonderful to support our brother.
We must follow the command of Jesus Christ
And remember to love one another.

The Lord is our Light and our Salvation.
We must realize that He is always near.
Let us tell of His goodness wherever we go.
We should tell it for others to hear.

We are men of God who are dwelling in unity.
We can sing praises to our Lord above.
Let the peace of God rule in our hearts
As He showers us with His endless love.

Men: Leading Others to Jesus Christ

We can say that we are leaders in the church.
This sounds as if it may be true.
But before we give ourselves this awesome title,
Let's be sure that Christ is leading us too.

The church will move in the right direction.
Christ is faithful to forgive our sin.
Where the church goes and what it does
Call for the dedication of Christian men.

There will be times when we receive compliments.
We will be given handshakes and positive nods.
Let us be careful not to get all puffed up,
Because the glory should go to God.

We can be leaders in our cities and towns.
We can be leaders wherever we roam.
But there is no leading that means as much
As the leadership we provide at home.

There are always tasks before us.
Society is keeping a watchful eye.
But who sustains us day after day?
Jesus is the one on whom we can rely.

No matter how heavy the load may be,
No matter how dark the night,
When we humble ourselves before the Lord,
He can make our burdens light.

As men, we are brothers in Christ.
Our Father is the Three-in-One.
We are heirs to the throne of God.
We can each be called His son.

He expects us to serve Him as the only Master.
He comes second to no one else.
We cannot send a substitute to face the Savior.
Each man must do this for himself.

We know Jesus gave His life for us.
We know He was crucified.
What have we done for Him, our Savior?
Of what have we been denied?

We cast our nets into the world.
We are successful only now and then.
Jesus can help us make a good "catch."
He wants to make us fishers of men.

There comes a time when we must change
And turn from the things we used to do.
We should put aside the old way of life
And adorn ourselves with something new.

We need to take time to check our pride.
Everything is not based on fortune or fame.
We may not be recognized by our usual identity
Because we now are wearing Jesus's name.

Yes, we are men leading others to Christ.
We must be strong and take a stand.
Let us thank our God and bless His name
For making each of us a man.

Men: Guided by God's Powerful Hand

As men who walk in the Heavenly Light,
We must follow, and we must lead.
We must follow the example of Jesus Christ.
We must help when there is a need.

We should follow His earthly example
As we live our lives each day.
It is the unconditional love of a Mighty God
That will help us along the way.

We have responsibility in the family.
The church needs our leadership too.
So we have to pray that God will guide us
About what He wants us to do.

Following Christ should be our goal.
We cannot put our trust in man.
It is the love of Jesus that will get us through.
We are guided by His powerful hand.

When will we hear His call for us?
Where shall we find the place?
Let Jesus point the way in our decisions
And then thank Him for His amazing grace.

There should be no mystery in our leadership
Or in being there for those we love.
Our families will not guess about where we stand
When our leadership comes from above.

Let's train our children in the way they should go.
Get them started on a path to stay.
Be there for them when they need us.
Let's keep them from going astray.

Oh, men of God, our spouses are virtuous.
They've been compared to precious stones.
As we travel on this journey to that promise land,
Love should flow throughout our homes.

God will give the final word.
Let us walk closely in the Father's tracks.
Let us say, in faith, during difficult times,
"There will be no turning back."

Getting Ready for Baptist Men's Day

Announcing the forthcoming Men's Weekend at Braddock Baptist Church

Baptist Men's Day is coming soon.
It's just a few weeks away.
We invite you to come and join us
As we worship on that special day.

In preparation for that celebration,
We are starting on Saturday night.
We'll have a Baptist Men's Soup Mission Supper.
There will be soups for your delight.

Steam will be ascending from every pot.
You won't have to raise your voice.
All you'll have to do is whisper,
And you may have the soup of your choice.

So when that special Saturday night rolls around,
Please bring something to help people survive.
Bring blankets, nonperishables, and toiletries.
You may keep someone in need alive.

Section IV

When Two People
Fall in Love

One Step from the Altar

Written especially for the wedding of Curtis Price and Linda Watson
Saint Louis, Missouri

As the flowers have been touched by the raindrops,
Falling so softly from above,
I have been touched by your affection
On this wonderful journey of love.

May we never be so far apart
That it could cause our love to grow weak.
Let us always share our lives together.
Let us hear each other when we speak.

It is such a pleasure to be in your presence.
I am captivated by your wonderful smile.
We are going to share a wonderful life
To the end of the very last mile.

We are headed for the altar, my love.
I can hear our wedding song.
The voice of Etta James is now proclaiming,
"At last, my love has come along."

We're getting closer to the altar now.
A great future is what I see.
I am ready to share my life with you.
Come and spend your life with me.

We are just one step from the altar.
Through our vows, we are taking a stand.
I promised that I would meet you here.
Now reach out and take my hand.

Please hold me in your heart forever.
I promise to do the same for you.
Let's take this one last step, my love,
As we prepare to say, "I do."

Come into My Life Forever

Dedicated to Bob Bogan and Irma Davis shortly after their wedding day
Alexandria, Virginia

Your love is my love from this day forward,
And my love is just for you.
We have made the decision to begin a new life.
This is what we were destined to do.

Your heart became mine on our wedding day,
And I gave my heart to you.
We both must handle each heart with care.
This is something I am committed to do.

We have agreed to share our lives forever,
Yet we shall still have a sense of self.
We don't have to stop being who we are
And try to become somebody else.

We have become one to share our hopes.
Come and let me dream with you.
Whatever the future holds for us,
God will be there to see us through.

Your wonderful world is now my world.
Our clouds have turned to skies of blue.
You have expressed your love for me,
And I have expressed my love for you.

We made a commitment at the altar.
I love you in a special way.
Some things come and then disappear,
But our affection will always stay.

Thank you for coming into my life.
My love for you is what I want to share.
We can thank God for blessing our future.
We now have this new life to share.

When You Came into My Life

*The author was commissioned by the bride and groom,
Russell Easter and Earnestine Psalmonds, to write and
present this poem as a toast at their wedding reception.
Alexandria, Virginia*

Earnestine Speaks

My dear Russell, you love to eat,
But there is one piece of advice you should heed.
Try to slow down when you're dining.
Stop swallowing your food at such high speed.

I know you cook excellent vegetables.
In the kitchen, you are ever so sweet.
You can probably do desserts and starches,
But the verdict is still out on preparing the meat.

You are a wonderful tenor who loves to sing,
But there is one thing I don't understand.
Why do you feel that if you're going to sing,
You must have the music in your hands?

Let the music go, and don't hold on!
Place the music down by your side.
An angel is likely to come along
And give you a musical ride.

You will make mistakes as you go through life,
But there is one thing going well for you.
That million-dollar smile and sense of humor
Will be an asset in whatever you do.

Russell Speaks

Earnestine, my darling, I'm aware of good health.
There can never be any doubt.
But you seem to get carried away
When it comes to working out.

You seem overly dedicated to exercising.
It's the most rigorous I have ever seen.
I may start with you but may not last
To the end of your long routine.

You take a lot of time to eat your food,
While the hour is just slipping away.
Sometime I wonder if dinner for you
Will continue into the next day.

You are an excellent chef, and I'm happy to say
That I know what delicious meals are all about.
I will be delighted to eat at home
Instead of always eating out.

Russell and Earnestine Speak (R = Russell; E = Earnestine)

R - From time to time I can be a bit tardy,
While punctuality is on your mind.
I can speed up when the occasion demands,
And that is something you will soon find.

E - As head majorette at Tuskegee University,
I was as flexible as a garden hose.
And one thing people don't realize
Is that I can still strike a majorette pose.

R - We both remember how we bonded.
It was while we were riding on a chartered bus.
We were on our way to a choir performance,
And there were things we had time to discuss.

E - We enjoy having fun and laughing together.
Now we are both wearing our wedding bands.
Let's face together the life ahead of us,
And let's keep on holding hands.

The Poet Speaks

While the sunset was painting the hillside,
Loneliness kept staining my heart.
The moment you came into my life
Was when I knew true happiness would start.

We have made a promise to love each other.
A new life is beginning today.
You love me, and I love you.
We want to always keep it this way.

Welcome, my love; you're a part of me.
And I have become a part of you.
We shall share in this new joy we've found.
May our best keep coming through!

You say I have made you happy.
I can say that you sustain my smile.
Let's allow nothing to come between us.
This is going to last for a long, long while.

Do You Know Whose Heart This Is?

You can't take my heart like that
And just slowly walk away.
You cannot do this on your own.
Shouldn't I have something to say?

That's my heart you're throwing around.
Does it really belong to you?
If so, please handle it with loving care,
The same way you used to do.

Please tell me where you're taking my heart.
Can't you see that I'm still here?
Since my heart and I want to be together,
You should leave it somewhere near.

Yes, I love you now, and I always will.
This is something you already know.
So you don't have to take my heart away.
I wish you would not go.

But take it away if you think you must.
Take it miles across the sea.
Wherever you take this heart of mine,
Please try to make room for me.

Extend a Welcome to Love

When you can see the trees smiling,
    stretching their fingers
    and reaching out to you,
    extend your arms and let them
    welcome you.

When the birds chirp and every
    sound seems to be a love
    song just for you, listen to
    them and let them tell you
    what you need to hear.

If you see a sign of compassion, or sense
    an atmosphere of comfort and delight,
    step forward and become the recipient
    of that which awaits you.

Encounter all that is reserved for you in a world
    where positive reservations don't always exist,
    unless you make them yourself.

Encounter love and claim that which is yours.
Recognize the one who loves you, and
    be careful not to miss claiming whatever
    that person has extended, just for you.

Love is bountiful but may not
    always flow toward you without
    someone to channel it in your direction.

Meet love; greet love; keep love.
    There will be good times.
    There will be bad times.

Embrace love, and let it be your constant companion
    through all times.

No Other Love

No other love could persuade me.
Nothing could make me change my mind.
I love you and want to marry you.
There is no one else to find.

I want us to become a family,
It's time for us to make a start.
I have always loved you for who you are.
Thanks for allowing me into your heart.

We know we should be together.
It will happen at the final "I do."
I don't want to be with anyone else.
My life will be spent with you.

I know you want to keep being yourself.
I have the desire to keep being me.
We just have to love each other
To make our marriage what it should be.

A Challenge to Young People

Opportunity Knocks but Will Not Break In

If you should hear opportunity knocking,
Be quick to allow accession.
If you don't, it will find another home
And deny you of a treasured possession.

Opportunity seems to be independent.
It doesn't stand around and cry.
If you don't accept it when you have a chance,
It is likely to pass you by.

You will have to listen for every knock.
You should extend a welcoming hand.
Opportunity will request to stay with you
But will not make any strong demands.

Permitting ingress is easy enough.
Just let this visitor come in.
Opportunity may come back in the future,
But there is no way for you to know when.

So treat opportunity the way you should.
Respond when you hear the knock.
Opportunity warns you of its desire to enter
But absolutely refuses to break your lock.

You, Too, Should Have a Dream

Dr. Martin Luther Jr. had a dream.
It has been repeated in a frequent refrain.
He saw the day when, among humankind,
Things would not continue to be the same.

Be recognized by the content of your character.
Be the best within your soul.
Don't simply develop character at the surface.
You are personally in full control.

You may have highest regards for this warrior.
You may marvel at the accomplishments he made.
But set out to make your mark in life.
As you remember the great price he paid.

Prepare yourself to meet new challenges.
This is a world where there is competition.
You have opportunities to make a difference.
You can improve this world's condition.

You are empowered to make decisions
About present and future situations.
Take your life and make the best of it
By working to enhance your education.

As you consider Dr. King's accomplishments,
Give some thought to what you can do.
Remember your dream and do not stop.
Until you see it all the way through.

Each year we celebrate Dr. King's life.
We honor him in a special way.
We should each recognize the hope
In the words he had to say.

Although he is gone, his dream still lives.
He is held in the highest esteem.
He was truly great but he was only one person.
You, too, should have your dream.

We are still honoring this great humanitarian
By the respect people wish to pay.
Think of the good that you can do in life,
And in the future, you may have your day.

A Breath of Danger

Satan blows wind of hurricane force.
He does it with a confident flare.
He blows a breath of danger.
You can smell it in the air.

He's out to see who is getting weak.
Who is disgusted with the Holy Word?
Who is finding fault with the Bible?
Who believes the gospel is absurd?

These are candidates whom Satan is seeking.
He is anxious to increase his list.
If there is anyone who has something for him,
This is the purpose for which he exists.

Don't let him breathe all over you,
No matter how forcefully he may exclaim.
Stand up to him with the Word of God,
And do it in the Savior's name.

Aim for the Sky

If you decide to aim for the sky,
You may not get all the way.
If you should aim for the ground,
That's exactly where you will stay.

You don't have to go to college,
But perhaps you would like to try.
You may decide to drop out of school,
And then you can watch others as they pass by.

A college education may be the first step
As you keep aiming for the sky.
What if you never get one?
Don't let it keep you from reaching high.

All of us know a number of people
Who have done well with no college degree.
Many opportunities in the years gone by
May no longer continue to be.

You can choose to aim for the sky,
Or you may wish to aim for the ground.
Please remember that if you aim low,
That is where you will always be found.

Getting yourself a good education
Could protect you from later regret.
If you want to accomplish your goals,
This is something you should get.

You need to keep aiming upward.
Let me tell you the reason why.
You don't ever want to fall too low,
Even if you do not reach the sky.

You Just Wait and See

The teacher said that I'm no good.
She said I'll never amount to a hill of beans.
I don't like going to her room.
I think she is awfully mean.

She never explains assignments well,
And we cannot say one word.
She usually speaks in a very soft voice,
But we had better pretend we heard.

The teacher says her work is important,
And you would think the school is small.
She gives homework as if she thinks
There are no other classes at all.

She says it should only take one hour
To do everything that she assigns.
It takes an hour to do one subject,
So I'm always two days behind.

One day, I'm going to be a teacher.
I am going to help all of the children learn.
If they don't understand everything I say,
They will at least know of my concern.

The teacher who said that I'm no good
Will have to apologize for all to see.
No one else can decide how good I am.
That decision is up to me.

My Soul Keeps Searching

My soul keeps on searching,
    looking for something that has not been found.
It keeps on longing for something,
    but the specifics are still unknown.

We often go searching.
Perhaps we are looking for a place
    where, all around us, there is happiness,
    unencumbered by negative influences.
Yet this something is still not within our reach.

Some situations in life seem to rise
    and take the focus away from
    all of our original plans.
They present obstacles that make us pause
    and take time to think about
    who and where we are.

We may do a complete inventory of relationships
    with friends, family,
    and others closest to us.

It could be that our souls are searching to understand
    everything in our surroundings.
This daunting task is one that, for us,
    earns a grade of incomplete or impossible.

My own heart seems to be longing for a world
    where people can know what it means
    to have respect for one another
    and still keep standing tall,
    because they know who they are themselves.

The road of life is often rough enough
    to interrupt one's well-planned journey.
We started with so much self-confidence.
Now life is trying to take us in a new direction.

Suddenly, we are traveling down the freeway.
We're headed somewhere unknown.
We simply know that it appears to be
    just opposite of where
    we had planned to go.

We can keep following that new path or
    cling to the road map with which we started.
We can continue down the first path or
    dare to experience that which is unknown.
The decision is up to us!

The encounters on the right path are sweet.
Greet them with a smile, and cherish them
    for as long as they will last.
Encounters that lead you down the
    path of destruction are bitter.
Greet them in a different manner,
    or they will try to follow you forever.

As your soul keeps seeking
    and your heart keeps longing,
    just be confident in the fact that
    someday you will have comfort in knowing
    you have arrived at your desired destination.

Sin Must Die

There is going to have to be a death
Before you can really begin to live.
So if you have finished existing in a world of sin,
You have your life to give.

Give it to Christ and let Him guide you.
Let Him lead wherever you go.
Let Him know you're willing to follow.
He is wiser than you can ever know.

You cannot keep existing in old surroundings.
You desire a life that is new.
You cannot just pretend to die.
This is something you have to do.

Be willing to give up your darkened past.
Tell Jesus what you want to be.
He has lifted others from the shackles of sin,
And He has a brighter day for you to see.

Section VI

Joy to the World!

An Approach to Christmas

I can feel the spirit of Christmas,
A time so dear to my heart.
This year, I'll take a new approach
As I decide just where to start.

I'll begin by thanking the Almighty God
For the gift of His Holy Son.
I'll thank Him for what He is doing for me
And the things He has already done.

As I begin this Christmas season,
I will think about the past.
What have I done for Jesus Christ?
When did I witness last?

What have I done for the Prince of Peace?
Why must I celebrate?
Will I lead someone to know His love,
Or will I let them continue to wait?

Christmas can bring a ray of hope,
Or it can bring us much despair.
Let us think about the loving Savior
Who keeps us in His care.

He came to us to be our Light.
So darkness should be cast aside.
Let Christmas be a time with Jesus as Lord.
Tell others how He provides.

Let's celebrate the birth of Jesus Christ.
He should guide us on our way.
His examples span from cradle to grave,
So let's honor Him on Christmas Day.

Celebrate the Light

People continue to walk in darkness
As if wandering in the middle of the night.
They cannot recognize the morning,
Because they do not see the Light.

Isaiah said, "A child is born.
The world has been given a Son."
These were words from the heart of a prophet,
And now the day has come.

Gabriel came to Mary with a message from God.
She would conceive and have a baby boy.
Since she had not known a man,
She was not filled with joy.

But there came a reassurance from Gabriel.
The Holy Spirit was in this plan.
This child would be the Son of God,
Not conceived by an earthly man.

Mary accepted this favor from God.
She knew that He had blessed her soul.
Her heart was filled with ultimate praise.
And now the story of His birth is told.

When the time came for the world to be taxed,
Mary and Joseph left Galilee.
She knew she would give birth to a Son
For the entire world to see.

The day arrived for the child to be born.
There are many places where this might have been.
But He was born in a lowly stable,
Because there was no room at the inn.

The angel told the shepherds about this child,
And the multitudes praised His birth.
He is the Savior of the universe.
Through Him there will be peace on earth.

All who heard this began to wonder.
There was amazement from the start.
But Mary, the mother of Jesus,
Pondered these things in her heart.

Now is the time for celebration.
Let us reflect on that wonderful night.
There are people still walking in darkness.
We must show them the Eternal Light.

Savior of the World

There was a time while Mary was engaged to Joseph
When she was too fearful to smile.
Although she was a virgin,
She was going to have a child.

Joseph could have embarrassed her.
He had the power right in his hands.
But he chose not to make this issue public,
Because he was known to be a just man.

Praise God for Joseph's decision on privacy.
Things were not as they may have seemed.
The child was conceived of the Holy Spirit,
As revealed to Joseph in a dream.

God told him Mary would have a son.
The prophet had foretold the same.
Mary would give birth to this wonderful child,
And Jesus would be His name.

Emmanuel, God with us!
The prophet foretold His life.
A trusting Joseph rose out of his sleep
And took Mary as his wife.

He treated her with kindness and loving care
While he waited for that special morn.
Be thankful for the Savior who loves us.
Remember the day when Christ was born.

God sent His Son to save the world.
Joseph was a man among all men.
The baby Jesus, now King of kings,
Was born to save us from sin.

Let's Celebrate the Holiday Season

This is the holiday season.
Family members are coming to town.
This is the time to be with others.
It's a time when love abounds.

Let's think about this season.
Let's cherish these special days.
We will gather for this annual occasion,
And we will celebrate in different ways.

Gifts will be exchanged around the fireplace.
Each package will be opened with glee.
Our hearts will be open to those around us.
How unforgettable this time will be!

This is a time to avoid complaining,
Which takes the fun away from it all.
We want to make this a cheerful season,
One filled with joy for all.

During this season, we renew acquaintances.
New people may enter our lives.
We will face the traffic as we rush to airports
To meet people as they arrive.

There may be time for all of our plans,
But we must schedule things without delay.
This is a time for celebration.
It's time for a holiday.

Fall in love, and laugh for a while.
Strengthen relationships to long remember.
Weddings take place through the year.
So it's okay in the month of December.

Go out shopping and write some checks.
Use plastic if that's what you must do.
But keep in mind that in a short while,
The bills will be coming to you.

Invite someone to go to the movies.
Listen to what they have to say.
These are the days of the modern era;
So it doesn't matter who decides to pay.

Buy something expensive to make an impression.
Watch someone's eyes begin to glow.
If you are not sincere about spending,
There is at least one person who will know.

Show coworkers a different side of you.
Honor them by doing something nice.
Keep on giving your honest opinion.
Keep giving unsolicited advice.

Always keep Jesus in the Christmas season.
Let us make it an occasion of worth.
Enjoy your blessings as you count them,
And let there continue to be peace on earth.

It's Just after Christmas

It's just after Christmas,
About three weeks or less.
And everything at home
Is still in a mess.

Decorations have come down,
But they are not put away.
I'll have more time tomorrow
Than I had yesterday.

I'll rearrange the furniture
And put the lights in a bag.
But picking up things
Just causes me to lag.

What about the dishes
That I hardly every use?
There is no place to store things.
Now that's real bad news.

Well, here come the bills
From my new credit card.
Why did I buy something
That makes me work so hard?

They said I could purchase
And have two months to pay.
Oh, but I made this purchase
Just after Thanksgiving Day.

Time sure does fly
And so does the money.
I wish every greenback dollar
Could be coated with honey.

I'm trying to think of something
That will make money last.
It would stick to my hands
Instead of going so fast.

What happened to Christmas?
I let it slip right by.
Now I'll have to wait a year
To give it one more try.

It's just after Christmas.
Guests and relatives have fled.
We can now settle down
And get back to our own bed.

That jolly ole Santa
Shouldn't have opened his sack.
It's just after Christmas.
I'm taking this stuff back.

It's just after Christmas.
I've got to make a new start.
I don't have any money
But a mighty big heart.

Happy Fathers' Day (HOPPY.)
JOHN PEDRO HOPKING

To a great Guy who comes
from the State that has

so much meaning
on its license Plate
& says "Smiling Face

& Beautiful Place"
You exemplify the guy
~~One of them~~;
with
the Smiling Face

yours

Hold on Tight to
Your Dreams!
Cause Dreams are made of
smiles & trials!

Stressed Spelled Backwards
is. Desserts

Apostasy =

Read about the Life of
Samson in Judges

PS. 37:25

Proverb 22,6

Jer. 6.16 ask for the O. Paths

I'll Fly Away -- Sing this Song
as I go to my grave at Arlington
National Cemetery - along side my
Husband JOHN PEDRO HOPKINS

The Capitol Hill Trilogy

The Capitol Hill Trilogy - Part 1

A Severe Case of FMD
(Foot-in-Mouth Disease)

A Washington politician made remarks in support of a segregationist.
He later regretted this and had to do a lot of explaining and apologizing.

You folks really should get off my case!
How much more of this can I take?
You act like I have committed a crime!
Can't I make one little mistake?

What I said couldn't hurt a thing!
I was speaking of 1948.
There was no malice in the tone of my voice,
And there was certainly no trace of hate.

The senator had reached one hundred years.
I was standing there by his side.
I wanted him to know I was quite like him.
We both shared our convictions with pride.

You are trying to make something out of this,
And it's because I'm from way down South.
Everybody who comes from my hometown
Does not insert both feet into the mouth.

I like blacks, and I think they're great.
Some of them are even smart.
They know I was speaking from my head
And not from my compassionate heart.

The rest of you should get over it!
I'm not planning to leave this town.
So don't count on increasing your side of the House,

Because I'm not planning on stepping down.

I know the importance of Affirmative Action,
And I just loved Dr. Martin Luther King.
If I could vote for a holiday right now,
That would be such an easy thing.

I didn't mean any harm by what I said.
So why don't you cut me some slack?
I can assist minorities if I stay in the Senate,
And my best friend from Georgia is black.

The Capitol Hill Trilogy - Part 2

I Need to Clear Up This Matter!

I can explain to you everything I said.
It's for sure, you can count on me.
I'm going to clear this whole thing up
During my confession on BET.*

I wasn't even talking about black people.
You reporters just got the wrong scoop.
I was referring to those awful terrorists
And some of these organized radical groups.

I have the feeling that you're not buying my story.
You're not trying to hear a word I say.
I believe I still have support in the Senate,
So I'll try convincing you another way.

---

*   Black Entertainment Television

The Capitol Hill Trilogy - Part 3

It Seems That I'll Have to Face the Music

Okay, if it makes you feel any better,
I'm giving up my powerful position.
It may do something for my side of the House,
But it's doing nothing for my diminished condition.

I'm doing all of this for the good of the country.
My party *will be* able to survive.
I'll be back home before the end of the year.
My constituents will greet me when I arrive.

Meanwhile, reporters, you listen to me.
I don't want you hanging around my home!
Don't you disturb anything near there!
You need to leave me alone!

Behind this, I'll face a lot of problems,
And I'm not looking forward to that.
If we need to talk about something in private,
Come to my office, and let's have a chat.

I would do anything to prove I'm serious.
I just need a little relief.
Reporters could not hound me any worse
If I were guilty of being a common thief.

For a long time, both colleagues and reporters
Have been trying their best to nail me.
If they were that jealous of my popularity,
Why in the world didn't they just tell me?

I want to turn this into something positive.
I hope you are willing to wait.
I'm going to do something to benefit blacks.
I want to also help my sovereign state.

Oh my! This thing is getting out of hand!
It's taking a brand-new twist, I see.
I will be gone, forgotten, and quickly replaced
By a rich young doctor from Tennessee.

You're no doubt wondering what lesson I've learned.
Well, making stupid comments just does not pay!
Here's my advice to you on freedom of speech:
You had better watch every last word you say!

Don't keep hammering on the things I do.
There are many issues that we must face.
But you're content to waste time doing nothing
While you try to put me in my place.

You just keep on asking questions.
You keep digging when there are no more worms.
When the American people backfire on you,
That's when you will begin to squirm.

Remembering Those Who Have Gone to Their Eternal Rest

A Tribute to Reverend
Dr. John O. Peterson Sr.

Man of God Called to Serve

The Bicentennial Committee of Alfred Street Baptist Church, Alexandria, Virginia, commissioned the author to write this poem for the Bicentennial Celebration (2003)

Thank You, God, for Your endless blessings.
Thank You for all that You have done.
Thank You for guiding Dr. Peterson's footsteps
In the Light of Your loving Son.

Thank You for helping him follow You, Lord,
And for being his guide along the way.
Thank You for Your protection, Dear God,
And for helping him remember to pray.

He has taken the gospel to other nations,
Where the people may have never heard.
He still stands before Your people
To share the promise of Your Holy Word.

He is a divine leader for those of his flock.
He has been with them through smiles and tears.
He has been a great organizer and visionary
While serving as pastor for thirty-nine years.

Now, Father, we ask for Your healing power
As he ministers in this earthly place.
Please touch him with Your hand of mercy.
Grant him the favor of Your continuing grace.

Please give him the strength to keep serving.
Sometimes his days seem a little too long.
You created him to be Your servant.
Bless him, Lord, and keep him strong.

He keeps You first on his Christian journey.
Witnessing has always been a part of his story.
Please keep Your arms of protection around him
Until he is called to meet You in glory.

Amen.

In Memory of Trayvon Martin

Whose Son Was Trayvon Martin?

Trayvon Martin was a seventeen year-old black teenager who was murdered by George Zimmerman on February 26, 2012, in Sanford, Florida. Zimmerman was acquitted July 13, 2013.

Whose son was Trayvon Martin?
In what state did he reside?
Was he a member of just one family?
Is that something you can now decide?

You can claim Trayvon as your son.
I can claim him as a son of mine.
His death sent black families searching
For answers they may never find.

Some of our sons are still alive.
But the same thing could have happened to them.
What did Trayvon do on that fateful evening?
Why did somebody start pursuing him?

Trayvon's death has added another chapter
To the profiling of young black men.
His death has written additional pages
In a chapter that should have never been.

What are you going to tell your children?
How can I explain this to the sons I love?
Can there ever be a safe place here on earth?
Or is the only shelter in heaven above?

Why can't a black man walk down the street
Without being suspected of committing a crime?
Will we ever be considered as just another person?
Will there ever be such a time?

You don't have to be a teenage criminal
To experience a lot of hurtful flak.
The only thing you have to do
Is to be found guilty of being black.

How many mothers must mourn such loss?
How many fathers must feel this pain?
When will black men be allowed to live
And achieve all they are destined to gain?

Whose son was Trayvon Martin?
Sanford, Florida, was not his only home.
He was a member of families all over this country,
Wherever you may choose to roam.

Trayvon's parents have set a peaceful example.
They have borne this burden with poise.
Other parents have also faced this tragedy!
When will they stop killing our boys?

The true story of Trayvon's death may never be told.
One side was presented by somebody else.
He was not around to tell the other side.
He was not alive to speak for himself.

How could a trip to the local store
Lead to such a horrible night?
How could a young man be shot to death
And have the killer end up being right?

It's hard for naked hands to compete with a gun,
So Trayvon's life came to an end.
The entire tragedy could have been avoided.
It didn't really have to begin.

There were witnesses for the prosecution.
There were witnesses for the defense.
Attorneys also presented their findings.
There was a jury that needed to be convinced.

Justice may not have prevailed in Sanford, Florida.
Many were disappointed when the verdict was heard.
Memories of Trayvon will remain forever,
And our Heavenly Judge will have the last Word.

In Memory of Lillie Braxton Kline

She Was a Mother to Hundreds Who Came

*Lillie Braxton Kline was the author's college dormitory
counselor, known then as Mrs. Johnson. After her marriage
to Earl Kline and moving to Las Vegas, Nevada,
her former students affectionately referred to
her as Mama Kline until her death.*

Mama Kline, we will miss your presence.
We were blessed by our time with you.
You showed love for others wherever you went,
As Jesus commanded us to do.

Everyone loved you for being so kind.
We loved because you were so wise.
We didn't have to tell you about our problems.
You could see them in our wandering eyes.

You knew when something was going wrong.
You could see it in our troubled faces.
Thank you for providing the guidance we needed
When we might have gone to dangerous places.

Mama Kline, you will forever be special.
Thank you for your loving smile.
You brought the joy needed in our college world.
All of us benefited from your friendly style.

You will be remembered by hundreds of students.
You gave us something that we cannot repay.
So some of us have gathered to say good-bye
And to be a part of your home-going day.

Although you never had children of your own,
You had two stepdaughters and still no sons.
You became mother to hundreds of men on campus
The day our college careers were first begun.

It was our first time living away from home.
Suddenly, our parents were not around.
We knew when we were placed in your care
What a wonderful new home we had found.

A Tribute to Loney Stewart

Willing to Help Somebody Else

*On the occasion of Loney Stewart's retirement from the
University of Maryland–Eastern Shore (UMES)*

We look forward to our retirement.
We do not have to wait forever.
But in those early years of one's employment,
It seems like that time is never.

Loney has given years of dedicated service.
As with everyone, times were good and bad.
This is a time for thoughtful reflection
On all of the good times that he had.

The years before arriving at UMES
Provided avenues for him to grow.
Lessons he learned during his employment
Are those the world may never know.

He wanted to continue to expand his horizon.
He was looking for ways to do more.
A great opportunity was presented to him
At the University of Maryland–Eastern Shore.

He worked patiently with the National Scholars
And with students in other programs too.
When it came to providing support for them,
This was something that he could do.

Loney was willing to accommodate others.
His attitude was "I'll let my own self be.
If I can help somebody else in life,
The Lord will take care of me."

And now that he has come to this special day,
We have gathered to show that we care.
Loney leaves fond memories at UMES
That we shall forever be able to share.

In Memory of Dixie Ree Hall Brooks

And Now She's Going Home

In memory of Dixie Ree Hall Brooks, the author's sister

Everybody knew her as Dixie,
Except all of her nephews and nieces.
They affectionately called her Aunt Dixie.
She showed love to them in great big pieces.

If you didn't spend time in her kitchen,
There is where you should have been.
You could get something to eat so quickly,
It could have been called "Dixie's Do-Drop-In."

You could come for hamburgers to order or pancakes,
Scrambled cheese eggs, waffles, or toast.
You could drop by for green-bean casserole,
A savory steak, or scrumptious pot roast.

She always had ice-cold Welch's grape juice.
Those Hungry Jack biscuits would flake just right.
She served the most delicious, crispy bacon,
And her pound cake was a tasty delight.

How could anyone forget her cookies and brownies,
Or her tempting German chocolate cake?
Her Waldorf salad would cause your mouth to water
While she was thinking of something else to bake.

All of us will miss the love she showed.
She was aunt, sister, cousin, and friend.
We knew we wouldn't have her forever.
Her life would someday have to end.

She was once the caregiver for others.
Thank God for a sister and her family's love.
God blessed her to be surrounded by those who cared
When she was called to that mansion above.

Dixie has been called to join the angels.
God has claimed her as His own.
She visited with us for eighty-three years,
And now she's going home.

Good-bye, Dixie! We love you!
Someday, we will join you around God's throne.
We are going to say farewell and let you leave,
Because we know you're going home.

*A Tribute to Jacqueline
Lamar Henry Green*

A Great Source of Musical Light

*Written for the eightieth birthday of Jackie Lamar Henry Green
at Alfred Street Baptist Church, Alexandria, Virginia*

This is a tribute to Jacqueline Lamar Henry Green.
For some, there is no need to say more.
Her life began on January 27 in Danville, Virginia,
In the year 1924.

She could have been identified by two initials
That are used for some children today.
Since she was a Baptist "preacher's kid,"
She may have been called a PK.

She moved to Alexandria, Virginia, when she was four years old,
And attended the Alexandria public schools.
Even then, she was a fun-loving person
And was considered to be somewhat cool.

She accepted her personal Savior at an early age.
She thought a life in Christ could be ever so sweet.
In nineteen hundred and thirty six,
She was baptized at Alfred Street.

She graduated from prestigious Howard University,
With a degree in music education.
She always knew, and so did everyone else,
That she would someday be a musical sensation.

She has taught private piano and voice lessons.
She has helped young people to see the musical light.
This has been her passion throughout her life.
She believes that helping others is right.

She has performed at concerts as a lyric soprano,
With a spirit that was a challenge to beat.
Every time she appeared for a grand performance,
She found audiences coming to their feet.

Jackie earned tenure at the Alfred Street Church.
She directed the Senior Choir more than thirty years.
She directed choirs for schools and other churches.
Perhaps she has experienced joy, frustration, and tears.

She has been a leader in the world of music.
She is an inspiration to associates and friends.
She founded the Jacqueline Henry Green Singers.
Her musical talent appears to have no end.

A music studio has been named in her honor.
There have been other recognitions too.
Musicians get experience in the Alfred Street Orchestra.
It will be invaluable their whole lives through.

The City of Alexandria noticed her accomplishments.
In every endeavor, she would do her part.
In 1990, she was honored by this historic city
By being appointed commissioner of the arts.

Jackie is one who likes to travel.
She has even ventured to the Holy Land.
On one of the tours, she had a serious question
About something she did not understand.

As the tour boat was crossing the Sea of Galilee,
Jackie was talking a lot and having a good time.
Suddenly, she turned to Dr. Peterson, looking puzzled,
With a serious question on her mind.

She asked, "Is this the same water that Jesus crossed?"
The pastor was constrained to answer, "Yes."
She quickly insisted that everyone become silent.
"Right now, we should be at our best!"

On a trip to Jordan, the tour bus arrived,
And the step up was constructed too high.
Jackie lay down in the door and pulled her feet inside.
The bus was not going to pass her by!

When she was seen eating bacon while in flight,
Jackie's rationale was both innocent and sweet.
She announced to the pastor, "This cannot be pork,
Because pork is something that I don't eat."

Finally, we should turn attention to fashion footwear.
She has paid the designers her dues.
If you could get a glimpse inside her closet,
You would discover hundreds of pairs of shoes.

So, Jackie, keep on stepping in the name of Jesus.
Keep serving Him in your Christian way.
We have come to show how much we care
In celebration of your eightieth birthday.

In Memory of Alvin Jerome Sydnor

His Soul Shall Dwell at Ease

Psalm 25:13
This poem is an interpretation by the author,
based on information provided by
Alvin Jerome Sydnor's nieces after his death.
His nieces are the narrators in the poem, which
was read at his home-going service.

Alvin Jerome Sydnor touched many lives,
And there is one thing that everyone learned.
Whatever he did was from his heart.
He was looking for nothing in return.

We left the South and moved to Washington,
But we never felt that we were alone.
Alvin knew that we were coming
And quickly welcomed us into his home.

He always told us, "I do the work around here,
But there is something that I want from you.
I want you to stay in school and give your best.
That is all I am expecting you to do."

Everyone came to Alvin for counseling.
He did not try to sugarcoat the truth.
He told each person exactly as he saw it
And this applied to both adults and youth.

He accepted all of us for who we were.
He was always like a daddy or a loving big brother.
He treated us as kindly as anyone could,
Whether father, grandparents, or one's own mother.

Alvin could always give advice about fixing cars.
He would say, "I know exactly what it takes."
I found that was true when my brake light appeared
While I was on a bridge with failing brakes.

I called Alvin, who told me to relax.
He said, "Tap the brakes, and ignore the clicking."
I overcame my fear of running off that bridge
And took it to him to get it ticking.

He worked tirelessly in his body shop.
Employees respected him for his wise advice.
He always had something positive to say.
He was recognized as being nice.

He loved his children, and he loved his wife.
He loved the church, as well.
He packed a lot into his years with us
And helped all of us to excel.

Alvin and each of us had something special.
It always came out in our conversations.
We accused each other of knowing everything.
It must have been a mutual admiration.

Psalm 25 was a source of strength for him,
Whether in Korea or helping family and friends.
He lifted his spirit and trusted in God.
He loved all of us until the end.

Celebrating Black History

Black History Month, Black History Week,
Call it whatever you will.
Blacks have made history year after year,
And there are those who are making it still.

Does this history come from great things done?
Or from the human sacrifice?
There continues to be suffering and discrimination.
Who is willing to pay the price?

There are those who oppose every effort you make.
They may even stand in your way.
And after you are placed below the cold, cold dirt,
They find a lot of nice things to say.

History is all about the past,
But it gives a glimpse of what lies ahead.
We should recognize people for what they do.
We sometimes ignore them instead.

Some things in history give us hope.
Some of it saddens and causes fear.
Blacks were struggling in the past,
And many of the obstacles are still right here.

Section IX

A Tribute to People Who Are Making a Difference

Trilogy:
A Tribute to President Barack Obama

The Barack Obama Trilogy, Part 1

Why Do You Hate Him So?

There are some people who seem to hate President Obama.
They have never openly expressed why they hate him.

You show him no respect as president.
Seemingly, it's because he's from another race.
Therefore, you think it shows political etiquette
To point your finger right in his face.

Oh yes! He is the president!
And you are an official in your own state.
But that does not begin to legitimize
All of those outward signs of hate.

You were in the chamber for the state of the union.
And without having a good reason why,
Right in the middle of the president's speech,
You blurted out that he was telling a lie.

You could have done it more discreetly,
As you continued to sit there and pout.
But you had to make sure it was audible.
Perhaps that's why you decided to shout.

There are others who completely agree with you,
Because the race issue comes from deep within.
You felt that you had to spit it out,
Thinking it would help your party win.

You have tried to deny his American citizenship.
You say he was born in another land.
Hawaii is now one of the fifty states,
Which you don't seem to understand.

Birth certificates serve as living proof.
That's what you wanted to see.
The president produced his with an official seal,
And you still couldn't let it be.

You had to keep on sounding uneducated
And spreading erroneous information.
Every time you had political discourse,
This was part of your conversation.

Some people need to pinch themselves
To see if their breathing is still intact.
He *is* president of the United States,
And this is a natural fact.

He was not elected with a disclaimer.
He fought the odds twice and won each race.
Now give him the respect that he deserves,
And get used to seeing that colorful face.

When you should have been trying to help the nation,
You appeared to have been taking it apart.
You wanted him to be a one-term president,
And that was the only thing in your heart.

You kept talking about having to save the nation.
You kept saying you've got to take it back.
To what new world are you taking it?
And will it include anyone who is black?

You say President Obama is the food-stamp president.
You keep saying he made the economy worse.
Look at where things were before he arrived
And see how he lifted America above that curse.

You tried your best to destroy the health care plan.
On that official law, you continued to pound.
You didn't care how you got your way,
Even if you had to close the government down.

You succeeded in causing people to be out of work.
Some of you even thought that was funny.
It's no laughing matter with a family and bills to pay
And somebody's playing with your hard-earned money.

You criticized the president for every decision.
Cooperating was something you just couldn't do.
All of the blame cannot land in the Oval Office.
Some of it is going to land on you.

The Barack Obama Trilogy, Part 2

Yes, Things Are Getting Better

Looking back to the day President Obama
arrived in the Oval Office in 2009

When he arrived in the Oval Office,
The economy was a complete disaster.
You thought as soon as he was sworn in,
It was something he should quickly master.

It took a number of years to dig that hole.
But you expect him to rush us out.
You don't seem to understand the reality,
So you are content to show your clout.

Every time he tries to make a little progress,
There is somebody from the "Party of No"
Trying to ensure that he is a failure
By blocking where he's trying to go.

Why are you so down on him?
You've had many years to squawk.
But you continued to remain silent,
And now you're ready to talk.

You spent money on other wars,
Weapons of mass destruction were your excuse.
And since they still have not been found,
Investment in that battle was of little use.

Jobs were being lost when he arrived.
That "sucking sound" was taking jobs overseas.
Now you want him to work a miracle
And clear up somebody else's bad deeds.

When the terrorist struck in New York City,
You came forward with leadership praise.
When Katrina hit, you were very patient,
Although that disaster lasted for days.

But everything that happens on his watch
Is reviewed through a microscope.
You keep stirring up doubt in the minds of people,
As if you want to see them lose all hope.

You couldn't care less about people's health.
So you tried to block his health care plan.
In your heart, you know it's good,
But you refuse to take a positive stand.

Wall Street and banks were extremely careless.
Handling their business was not at the top.
Wiretapping Americans was going on then,
And torturing people had to be stopped.

There have been questions about his name.
You have posed questions about his birth.
There are negative comments about his faith
And everything else that is on this earth.

I think somebody has finally awakened.
Let's move together now; it's time to start.
This country is home to all of us.
We should keep it close to all of our hearts.

Try to focus on the good he is doing.
United, we can pass the test.
He will keep serving the American people.
He can offer you no more than his best.

Some of you are blatantly disrespectful,
Referring to him by only his last name.
You have addressed others as "the president."
Why can't he be addressed the same?

You have felt great with your guns at rallies.
You have thrown things you claimed were gifts.
Why couldn't they be passed to him with decency?
Why is there such an obvious shift?

He has been accused of not being tough enough.
You say he should be more of a man.
He has sense enough to think things through,
Something else you fail to understand.

He has been criticized for every action.
His confidence is as high as a steeple.
He will be remembered as a great president,
So he's going to serve the American people.

The Barack Obama Trilogy, Part 3

I'm Trying to Do My Job

President Obama pressed forward when some people seemed determined to ensure that he would not be reelected for a second term. This is the author's poetic imagination of what the president was thinking about the election.

You have dragged me through the sticky mud.
You have dragged me through the clay.
You have done everything possible to belittle me.
Now there is something I have to say.

I am not leaving the White House.
I have no plans to post a sign.
You may think you have it all worked out.
You think you have a perfect design.

The people put me in this office.
And I know what this is all about.
I am not too naive to realize
That the people can put me out.

I can hear the voices of people speaking.
I hear voting citizens' personal cry.
When you ask who should lead them,
You will find that it is I!

So support me while I try to do my job.
This country also belongs to you.
I know how to lead the United States,
And it's something I'll continue to do.

No other leader has faced such scrutiny.
Probably no other person ever will.
I've answered questions from everybody,
And there are people who are hounding me still.

There will be plenty of time for me to see my errors.
You don't need to keep piling on.
I'm trying to get this country out of a mess
Caused by the harm that others have done.

It's true that things could be better.
I'm doing everything I can do.
I know I haven't reached perfection,
And, quite frankly, the same goes for you!

A Tribute to Reverend Dr. Howard-John Wesley

Celebrating in the Name of the Lord

*In 2008, Reverend Dr. Howard-John Wesley was installed as the eighth
pastor of the historic Alfred Street Baptist Church in Alexandria, Virginia,
founded in 1803. The author was commissioned by the Installation
Committee to write this poem for one of the installation weekend services.*

The Pulpit Committee prayed and went out searching.
With God's help, they would get the job done.
There were many candidates ready to answer the call,
But they were searching for the "chosen one."

They found a faithful servant and steward.
He was not out looking for fame.
He is now the pastor at Alfred Street.
Reverend Dr. Howard-John Wesley is his name.

The congregation elected him in 2008.
April is when his pastorate began.
His wonderful family accompanied him
As supporters of this God-sent man.

The Installation Committee and its subcommittees
Planned events that all will remember.
Volunteers started working during the month of May
For an installation at the end of September.

There were twenty days of prayer and worship services.
There was a cookout and carnival—and pizza with the pastor.
The Installation Service and the Concert of Praise
Honored Pastor Wesley and glorified the Master.

The pastor has succeeded in a number of areas.
He has confidence that never fades.
However, at the cookout on September 7,
He met his match in a game of spades.

The Subcommittee for Hospitality and External Affairs
Reached out to the pastor's family and friends.
Organizations and institutions could participate
In the joy that seemed to have had no end.

The *Souvenir Journal* is worthy to be cherished.
Names and ads were inadvertently omitted.
The committee requested everyone's sincere apology.
Through Christ, they should be acquitted.

Pastor Wesley, you are now installed to lead this flock.
Dr. Peterson passed the baton to you.
God blessed you by bringing you to Alexandria.
Keep trusting and He will guide you through.

A Tribute to Reverend Dr. Faye Savage Gunn

This Precious Jewel We Have Found

On the occasion of Reverend Dr. Faye Savage Gunn's
retirement as former pastor and assistant minister at Alfred
Street Baptist Church in Alexandria, Virginia

Speak of a beautiful orchid from a flower garden.
Talk about a lily from the valley of the sun.
Then think about the sweetheart of Alfred Street,
And focus your eyes on Reverend Dr. Faye Savage Gunn.

She is a woman of wisdom and understanding.
She is a pillar of strength in every way.
Dr. Gunn serves the Lord through service to others,
And He keeps blessing her day after day.

She has been recognized as a woman of courage.
She has a heart for helping people in need.
Because of her dependence on the Power of God,
She has stepped forward when it was time to lead.

Dr. Gunn has been at hospitals early in the morning.
She has prayed with members before their operation.
She has stood by the bedside of dying loved ones
As a source of comfort and consolation.

Dr. Gunn has studied to show herself worthy.
Her many degrees have prepared her to teach.
The Holy Spirit controls her daily life,
And now the world knows that she can preach.

A lot of women say they are "queen of the kitchen."
For some dishes, they may be leader of the pack.
But when it comes to making sweet potato pie,
Those wannabe cooks had better stand back!

Trying to welcome Pastor Wesley to Alfred Street,
One sister baked a sweet potato pie—in a flash!
Word is out that Pastor Wesley took one bite
And quickly threw the rest of it in the trash.

Faye came to the rescue and saved the day!
After tasting *her* pie, there could be no doubt.
We knew he was happy when he smacked his lips
And said, "Now that's what I'm talking about!"

Faye is a connoisseur of the finest food.
But if you want to really hear her taste buds sing,
Just bring her one or two hot yeast rolls
And a plate loaded with chicken wings.

The entire congregation knows who drives Miss Daisy.
When out on the highway, just turn your head.
If you see a black Mercedes go zipping by,
That's probably Miss Daisy who is driving her husband, Fred.

She knows how to buy her clothes and shoes.
She may go shopping and stay awhile.
When Faye is not wearing that gospel robe,
This is one preacher who dresses in style.

When the occasion dictates dressing up,
Take those flat shoes out of her sight.
Faye struts out wearing at least three-inch heels,
Whether it's on a Sunday or a Friday night.

If you go to Dr. Gunn's office to discuss a problem,
You had better be ready to stand the test.
Don't try to give her just half of the facts.
You may as well prepare to share the rest.

She will not stand for beating around the bush.
She is not going to guess what you are trying to say.
She is willing to help you if you're sincere,
And she does it in such a caring way.

She is going to tell you exactly like it is!
And it's all right if you get bent out of joint.
Because of her honesty and profound integrity,
She feels constrained to get right to the point.

Alfred Street is going to miss this wonderful angel.
We can rejoice that she will still be around.
We thank God for blessings us all these years
With this precious jewel that we have found.

Farewell, Dr. Gunn, from all of us.
We pray that God will bless you in whatever you do.
We know that you will be praying for us,
And we will certainly keep praying for you.

A Tribute to Mrs. Ruby Geraldine Hall Williams

A Mother's Love Comes Shining Through

Celebrating the eightieth birthday of Ruby Geraldine Hall Williams,
the author's sister

We have gathered for a grand celebration.
We have come here for a special occasion.
Mrs. Williams was excluded from the planning,
But it took some strong persuasion.

If this had all been left up to her,
She would have planned it all by herself.
Sometimes she is such a super mom;
She doesn't need help from anyone else.

But just when she started to give her opinion,
She met her firm but friendly fate.
Her daughter said, "I'm in charge of this!"
And she immediately stepped up to the plate.

She said, "You've been doing for everyone else,
And this is your very special day.
If you don't mind, I'll handle this.
So kindly step back, and I'll do it my way."

It wasn't easy for the birthday lady,
But she accepted the challenge with pride.
She agreed to let others do everything.
It was hard for her to step aside.

She said she didn't know what was going on.
Only a little information got to her in sparks.
She was not completely in the light
Or totally in the dark.

This is a wonderful birthday tribute
To the person we respect so much.
If she is anywhere in the world and there's a phone,
She is always going to keep in touch.

If she invites you into her home for a delicious meal,
You should sit down and be prepared to stay.
As long as there is food anywhere near,
She is going to keep bringing it your way.

This is one way of showing her hospitality.
She is one of the finest hostesses in town.
If good eating is what you are looking for,
She is the one person you should hang around.

She shows love for all of her children.
There is nothing reasonable that she wouldn't do.
She proves that her love is unconditional,
As a mother's love comes shining through.

We cannot explain all the joy it brings
When the grandchildren come to her mind.
She has a special place in her heart for them.
It is a reservoir of love that all can find.

They know their grandmother cares for them.
They have never had reasons to doubt.
They return that love in different measures.
That is what family is all about.

Her children's spouses are welcome additions.
She considers them as her family too.
Her grandchildren's spouses are her grandchildren.
Everybody is a part of her crew.

Mother Williams is devoted to the work of God.
Time and resources are something she can give.
She knows that God's people and His church
Are a part of the life she lives.

So as friends and family, we are here for you.
We have shared with you in laughter and tears.
We celebrate how God has blessed you
For all of these eighty years.

This is your day, and we honor you.
Let all of us rejoice together.
You have stood by us, and we'll stand by you
Through both stormy and sunny weather.

A Tribute to Honorable Judge Greg Mathis

All Rise for Judge Greg Mathis!

This is a tribute to an excellent judge
Who is filled with compassion right to the brim.
He tries his best to help young people
When the chances are remarkably slim.

He can think of a way to encourage the litigants.
He can also put them right in their place.
It matters not how long they have been on drugs.
He can look them in the face.

He can compare his life with some of theirs.
He has experienced spending time in jail.
He compliments those who are now in rehab.
If they lie about it, he can always tell.

This is a judge who knows what's going on.
It seems that he is guided from above.
He believes in discipline for wandering souls
With something he calls tough love.

He willingly reflects on his personal life
And how he was once standing in their shoes.
He doesn't mind giving reality checks
To some of those who are crying the blues.

I'm talking about a judge who tries to be fair.
He tries to lift parents who have fallen too far.
Don't enter his courtroom trying to be a diva.
He will remind you that you are not a star.

He likes to see families try to come together.
He often encourages reconciliation.
Absentee mothers and deadbeat fathers
Are reminded of their obligations.

People everywhere should know Judge Mathis.
Standing before him brings laughs and tears,
He may rule against you, but the lesson learned
Can lead to success in the coming years.

Under This Canopy of Happiness and Sorrow

Light Skin versus Dark Skin

Did she succeed because her skin was light?
Does she think she is better than you?
Do you have a reason to think that way?
What has she ever done to you?

You say he failed because his skin was dark.
Is that really what was holding him back?
Was he at work when he should have been?
Or do you remember when he became too slack?

The persons with dark skin faced many problems.
Those with light skin faced problems too.
They were often called names they did not deserve.
This is what some people like to do.

Light skin, dark skin. Dark skin, light skin.
Is this as far as the human eye can see?
Should we exert this energy on the outside shade?
Or could a glimpse inside help discover the key?

Don't try to belittle people you see
Just because their complexion is light.
Don't go making snide remarks
When you don't even know their plight.

And just because a person's complexion is dark,
Doesn't give you a license to go poking fun.
Perhaps each of you can be proud of your color
As you continue enjoying God's beautiful sun.

He Wouldn't Take Time to Listen

He's doing no good down here on earth.
It seems that he's about to leave and get moving
    to wherever he happens to be going.

People tried to break the rocks of his heart.
All efforts were completely in vain.
Friends tried to tell him that he was driving
    in the wrong lane,
      the one leading to nowhere.

He ignored his parents, the pastor,
    and all of those do-gooders
    at the church, at school,
    and in the community.

Now he's in trouble with the law.
He's in trouble with his family.
He's out of favor with God and man.
And it's all because of one critical thing:

    He just wouldn't take time to listen.

Can't You See That She Is in Need?

Can't you see that she's in need?
Have you observed that
    everything around her is falling,
    one level at a time?

Nothing is going right, and
    no one seems to care.
She's in pain; her heart is breaking.
Yet nobody seems to be concerned
    about what is happening.

Should she jump up and scream?
Should she wave a flag saying Help?
Her problem seems to weigh heavier
    than the sound of screaming.

She needs more than a waving flag.
If you have the ability to help
    but your desire is somewhere else,
Follow your desire, because
    You could be dangerous for her.

You talk about her,
    but you refuse to talk with her.
You spread your affection around her,
    but no showers of your compassion
    have fallen on her.

You are a great observer.
You see everything that is right or wrong
    with the world.
In all of your wisdom, you can analyze
    any person or any situation.

So now that you see she's in need,
What are you going to do about it?

My Eyes Are Fountains of Tears

Now I bitterly weep because
My sorrow continues to increase.
The pain is severe, and the burden is heavy.
My eyes have become fountains of tears.

The streams are gushing forth.
They are moving faster than
Water from a power-driven well.
And nobody has seen them flow.

Who cares besides me?
Who feels my sorrow?
Will anyone stand with me,
Or will friends and family just go away?

My mistakes in life are mine.
Your mistakes in life are yours.
You can fight your battles, and
I can fight my battles.

We can fight our battles together, or
We can both trust in God.
If we remain obedient to Him,
He will fight our battles for us.

I want to give in to the Savior who said
He will be with us always.
He has never lost a battle, and
He will not lose this one.

These fountains of tears will cease to produce.
The rushing waters will cease to flow!
Then we can consider the battle finished!
In Him, we are victorious.

Praise God!

Be Careful Where You Store Your Treasures

Where will you store your treasures?
Where will you store your fears?
Perhaps you could place them over there,
Right beside your stream of tears.

Think about what joy can bring.
Try to focus on a brighter day.
You should look into the future,
Because the past has gone away.

What if you should move your treasures
From beneath the canopy of shame?
Store them in another place
That represents your good name.

Weariness and pain are often present.
They know how to get in your way.
Sadness and disgust may wander in,
But you don't have to let them stay.

Joy and happiness are promised.
You need to claim them as your own.
What a wonderful gift from our Father,
Who sits on His heavenly throne.

Employ goodwill and understanding.
Insist on letting hateful thoughts go.
Store your treasures in the right place,
And watch your blessings grow.

Wars Over There versus Wars Over Here

There is a lot of talk about
    dodging the draft,
    avoiding the war, or
    getting involved in war.

A beautiful exchange of rhetoric continues to flow
    concerning serving where needed,
    responding to the call, and
    being where one ought to be.

There is still talk about
    serving in the war in South Korea,
    avoiding the war in Vietnam,
    and being proud of the wars now ended.

Yet veterans are still suffering from personal pain
    caused by their involvement in these wars.
There is talk about
    encounters on the battlefield.
There is talk about
    attacks and retreats.
There is talk about
    victories and defeats,
    lives lost, and friends saved from the blast.

Victory! Victory! Victory!
Yes, there is talk about victory.
This war was won.
That war was won.
This war was over there.
That war was somewhere else.

Energy has so long been devoted
      to wars over there!
But what about the wars over here?
What about the war on crime?
What about the war on drugs?
What about the wars on
      poverty, homelessness,
      illiteracy, and hunger?
What about all of the street wars?
Who is going to fight these battles?

Somebody is definitely dodging the draft!
Somebody is dodging responsibility.
Somebody is failing to do anything about
      the thousands of unfriendly soldiers
      approaching from every side.

Somebody is avoiding the criminal commanders
      on the streets of our cities.
They are those who come to battle
      with forceful battalions.
They are physically trained,
      mentally prepared,
      and financially supported.

Somebody is avoiding
      a face-to-face confrontation
      with street commanders in our communities.
These street forces are strongly determined
      to wipe out our youth,
      to sweep away the elderly—in body and spirit,
      to push the hungry and the poor
      further into the deep, dark pit of despair.

It is not victory for those who suffer!
Instead, it is a great imposition on some
who are already standing at an
uncomfortable status in their lives.

Yes, the war is still on
among the people in our communities!
Their battle is not over.
They are still fighting to survive.

There can be no surrender!
There can be no thoughts of resting
on previous accomplishments.

We cannot stop and tally what we have done
Until these domestic wars are also won.

What Color Is the Loss of Life?

There are things we don't like about America,
But we are here to stay.
This country belongs to all of us,
And we have come a long, long way.

What color is death in America?
What color is the loss of life?
Why must so many leave this world
Because of a gun or knife?

How many more parents will mourn
At the funeral of a girl or boy?
Why must their day be filled with sorrow
When it should be filled with joy?

Who can stop the senseless killing?
Will there ever be and end?
Instead of seeing their children grow up,
Parents have to imagine what they may have been.

It has been said that guns don't kill,
But people kill by using a gun.
It really doesn't matter how it's said;
Death is nothing that concludes in fun.

Who is going to tackle this problem?
How long will this epidemic rage?
When will there be an end to the killing?
Will we ever turn a bulletproof page?

Can you help in this critical battle?
Is there anything you can do?
Right now, the problem belongs to somebody else.
Someday it could be resting on you!

Enjoying This Planet Called Earth

What do we possess on this planet called Earth?
What did any of us create?
It would be fair to answer, "Nothing at all!"
We cannot prove that it was any date.

We are walking under God's beautiful sky.
We're walking on His earth.
We've been breathing His life-sustaining air
Since the moment of our birth.

We can't make the trees stand up.
We can't make them wave their arms.
None of us can cause the rivers to flow
Or make the crops grow on the farms.

Nothing on earth is under our control.
We have no reason to boast.
We should be grateful for this planet called Earth
Because we're likely to benefit most.

Let us keep enjoying this planet called Earth.
We must remember that it is God's creation.
We can't take credit for anything
When we're involved in conversation.

I Wish Those Clouds Could Be Dust

When I look at the clouds,
I wish they could be the dust from my feet
    as I fly away to heaven.
I visualize leaving all the cares of this world
    right here on earth.

As I ascend higher and higher,
    the clouds grow larger and larger.
I see the dust rising and spreading
    throughout the world.

Surely, someday I'll fly away,
    and I'll rise above the clouds.
I'll rise above the dust.

The earth will not rise with me.
It will remain as the anchor.
I will continue to ascend.
I will leave the dust and the clouds behind.

CPSIA information can be obtained at www.ICGtesting.com
Printed in the USA
BVOW02*2045040215

386241BV00001B/52/P